ONE HUNDRED PERCENT MARRIAGE

Bisi Adewale

Edited by Agbeleye Oladele (08033538725)

ONE HUNDRED PERCENT MARRIAGE

By

BISI ADEWALE
Copyright (c) 2008

Published by
Living Home Ventures
Ajoke Plaza (1st floor) 525 Agege Motor Road,
Ladipo /Alasia Bus-stop
Beside Majok Petrol Station
Oshodi, Alasia Lagos, Nigeria
E-mail: familybooster@yahoo.com
Website: www.familybooster.com,
Blogsite:www.bisiadewale.com
Tel: +2348056457013; 8068312004, 8051512823.

FIRST WORD

YOUR MARRIAGE IS WHAT YOU MAKE OF IT

How healthy is your marriage? Are you happy in it or tired of it? If you're tired, who is to blame? Do you say your spouse, in-laws, friends, poverty, your job or lack of it? You may not like these questions, but I would tell you the truth - your marriage is what you make of it.

You are the number one friend or foe of your marriage. You determine what happens in it; you can either make it better or destroy it.

A wise young boy heard about the wisest old man in another region. The boy decided to meet the old man, to prove to the man that he, the young boy, was the wisest. He challenged the old man to a contest when he got there. He told him that there was neither a riddle he could not solve nor a proverb he did not understand. He further brazenly announced that there was no question he could not answer easily, stressing the certainty of his ability to do all things.

The wise old man gave him a piece of chalk and told him to draw the natural lines on the palm of his hands. The boy quickly did that, effortlessly. The wise old man looked at it and saw that he had drawn the lines on his left palm. He said that he had expected him to draw the ones on the right, hence he failed. Though the boy protested, the old man said that following instructions was part of the test. He then concluded by saying, "When I asked you to draw the lines on your palm, you were supposed to have asked, "Which of the palms' should I draw, left or right?"

Having failed the test, the young boy wanted to prove that the old man could also fail his test. He held a bird in the palm of his hand, hid it behind his back and asked the old man if it was dead or alive? "The old man looked at him, shook his head, laughed a little and said, "It is in your hand whether alive or dead. If it is alive and I tell you it is, you can squeeze it and it dies; so either dead or alive it is in your hand."

Your marriage is the bird. I am saying that it is in your hands. IT IS WHAT YOU MAKE OF IT. IT IS ENTIRELY IN YOUR HANDS TO DECIDE

EITHER IT WILL LIVE OR DIE. THE CHOICE IS YOURS.

Many factors can affect your marriage negatively but none stronger than your attitude, actions, reactions, inactions, selfishness, thoughts and busy schedule. Besides, indecision, bad attitude toward prayers, immaturity, unfriendliness and fear; attachment to the past, secrecy, laziness, pride, bad communication and crisis management skills affect your marriage deeply. Again, improper mentality, inordinate ambition, bad character and incoherently expressed expectations can shake your marriage too. The last set - rigidity, self-glory, self-justification, self- judgment, unilateral decision, wrong association, wrong information are as extremely dangerous in marriage as the previously stated factors.

Any other thing life throws at a marriage is an external attack. It can be destroyed by the joint efforts of the couple no matter how difficult. But WHEN IT IS A WAR WITHIN, IT IS A WAR INDEED. When a couple fights each other, they do not tear clothes; rather, they tear flesh. They do not shed water; they shed blood. INTERNAL CRISIS DESTROYS EXTERNAL GLORY.

A piece of land left uncultivated becomes a wilderness. In the same way your marriage becomes a 'wasteland' if you fail to work at it. No marriage works on its own. It is also like a car; somebody must be at the driver seat, controlling the steering.

So making your marriage work is a task that must be done. Nobody will do it for you. It is your responsibility. I will teach you in this book what you need to do to make it work.

CHAPTER 1

WHAT MANNER OF MARRIAGE IS YOURS

Before you go further into this book, I want you to check your marriage on the scale of 1-100. How will you rate yourself? Besides, how will your spouse rate the marriage? Before you answer that, kindly answer the following questions sincerely and score yourself.

Be thou diligent to know the state of thy flocks, and look well to thy herds (Proverbs 27:23)

HEALTHY MARRIAGE TEST
1. Have you said "I love you" to each other in the past one week? Yes   No
2. Do you sleep in the same room?
3. Has somebody come to settle any dispute for you in the last 3 years?
4. You've not argued about sex in the last one year?

5. You've prayed together in the last 48 hours.

6. You say "I am sorry" regularly to each other.

7. You know each other's shoe size?

8. The husband knows the wife's bra sizes?

9. You hug each other every day?

10. You have never had a shouting match?

11. The wife invites the husband for sex?

12. You know each other's salary?

13. You know each other's e-mail password?

14. You've looked at your wedding pictures together in the last one year?

15. You discuss freely about your sex life?

16. You love each other more than your family members?

17. You take a stroll together?

18. You plan your annual vacation to be in the same period?

19. You have a joint bank account?

20. You both have your names on the documents of your car and landed property?

21. You attend the same church?

22. You go to church together?

23. You often go to social gatherings together?

24. You walk hand- in- hand on the street?

25. The man helps the wife in the kitchen?

26. You praise each other in the public?

27. You easily show your affection in the public?

28. You are each other's confidant?

29. You are each other's best friend?

30.Can you answer each other's phone calls?

31.You have sex regularly without quarrels?

32.Nobody is closer to you (your mother, friends and children inclusive) than your spouse?

33. You easily share your joy and fear?

34.You don't enjoy it when your spouse travels?

35.You rarely quarrel about money?

36.You never go to bed without settling your differences?

37.You eat together?

38.You create time just to be together?

39.You bath together regularly?

40.You call each other pet names?

41.You wash each other's under wear?

42.You have time to dance together?

43.You've read marriage books in the last two months?

44.You rarely have misunderstandings about in-laws?

45.You kiss regularly?

46.You massage each other's body regularly?

47.You sleep in each other's arms regularly?

48.A times you sleep naked beside each other?

49.You discuss joyfully when you make love?

50.People around you know that you are very close?

51.You celebrated your last wedding anniversary?

52.You celebrated your spouse's last birthday in a special way?

53.You buy special gifts for each other regularly?

54. You laugh and crack jokes together regularly?
55. You enjoy each other's hobbies?
56. You attend your children's end of the year party in their school together?
57. If you have the chance to re-marry, you will marry your spouse?
58. You know all your spouse's colleagues by name?
59. You go to your spouse's office?
60. You evangelize together?
61. You have family altar regularly?
62. You never argue in the presence of your children?
63. You pray for your spouse regularly?
64. You believe you did not marry wrongly?
65. The wife is fully submissive?
66. The man is a lover boy?
67. You attend marriage seminars regularly?
68. You have many marriage tapes and CD's?
69. You watch and listen to marriage CD's and tapes regularly?
70. You can say the husband is a servant-leader?
71. You can say the wife is a good follower?
72. The man appreciates the woman after eating the food she cooks?
73. He appreciates the wife's dressing?
74. He appreciates her outlook?
75. He appreciates the woman after sexual intercourse?

76. The woman appreciates the man after paying the children's school fees, house rents and electricity bills?
77. The woman thanks the man for eating her food?
78. The woman appreciates her husband's outlook?
79. Ever said "thank you for marrying me"?
80. The man admits it when he is wrong?
81. He never forces the wife to have sex with him?
82. Does not avoid his responsibility because the woman denies him sex?
83. Do you visit a counselor together during a misunderstanding?
84. Have never allowed a third party to come between you?
85. Can you say your marriage is a model?
86. You celebrate each other's parents?
87. You celebrate each other's family?
88. You do everything together?
89. You call each other regularly from the office just to say hello?
90. Ready to make any sacrifice to make each other happy?
91. You miss your mate sorely when he or she is not around?
92. You spend at least two hours per day talking intimately together?
93. You reach orgasm regularly in your sex life?
94. You spend at least thirty minutes in foreplay regularly before sex?

95. You can use the word FULFILLED for your marriage?

96. You can use the word INTIMATE for your marriage?

97. You can use the word HEALTHY for your marriage?

98. You play together?

99. Have gone on a prayer retreat together more than once?

100. You can use the word ROMANTIC for your marriage?

Now, count how many "Yes" answers you made. What did you score? Is it up to 50 per cent? Halleluyah, if you score up to 80 per cent! What a great marriage you have! But, remember you scored yourself. What if I take 30 marks away from your scores and I call it "sincerity marks", (marks that I keep to myself to cover for the answer you gave without being sincere), then what do you think you still score?

So whatever you score, deduct 30 from it, the remainder is your real score. Do you now see that you still have a lot of work to do on your marriage? Be ready to do new things, as you will discover in this book.

CHAPTER 2

NINETY PERCENT IS NOT ENOUGH

Even if you had scored ninety percent in the healthy marriage test, it wouldn't have been enough. Hundred percent is your target. Your marriage should not deteriorate; it should improve and become better than when you initially got married.

But the path of the just is as the shining light, that shines ever brighter unto the perfect day (Proverbs 4:18)

You must continue to do what will make your marriage better, increase intimacy, and make your union   stronger.
No matter the state of your marriage, it can be better. You can turn your home into a paradise on earth. It is the will of God that you enjoy your marriage. He did not give you your spouse to punish you, he didn't bring you into that marriage to make you miserable; rather, he brought you there to make you happy.

And the Lord God said, it is not good that the man should be alone: I will make him a help meet for him (Genesis 2:18).

Marriage is for your good; it is to strengthen you, to make you strong and better. It is to establish you and make you what God has created you to be.

Two are better than one; because they have a good reward for their labour. For if they fall, the one will lift up his fellow; but woe to him that is alone when he falleth; for he hath not another to help him up. Again, if two lie together, then they have heat, but how can one be warm alone? And if one prevail against him two shall withstand him and a threefold cord is not quickly broken (Ecclesiastes 4:9-12)

I know you don't just want to be married; nobody does. You want to be happily married; you want to be with a man or woman that loves you, and you want to radiate the life of God. You do not want the honey moon period in that marriage to end; you really want to enjoy yourself. This is possible, yes; it is possible. It can happen. You can turn your home to a haven of love and tranquility. You can make your home to become the source of your joy. You can remove tension from your home and stop living as if you are in detention. There can be peace in your home; the war can come to an end. You can live without strife, bickering, resentment, nagging. You can truly enjoy your home. Ninety percent is not enough, therefore; your marriage can be the best.

CHAPTER 3
THE WONDERS OF A
HEALTHY
MARRIAGE

Beloved, I wish above all things that thou mayest prosper and be in health, even as thy soul prospereth (3John 2)

"Getting married is good, staying married is better, a healthy marriage is the best."

Here is an excerpt from a newspaper.

WOMAN WHO RAN OVER STREET REVELERS IS SENTENCED

A woman who injured 49 people when she plowed her car through a street festival while on crack cocaine was sentenced to 25 years in prison.

Tonya Bell apologized to the victims, many of whom testified how their broken bones, scars and psychological wounds from the June 2 incident had a profound impact on their lives, limiting their ability to work or pursue their life passions.

"I'm so sorry for the pain I caused", said Bell, who quivered at the defense table and wept often during the half-hour hearing. "It haunts me and I asked God to bring you back to health."

Bell, 30 of Oxon Hill, Maryland, pleaded guilty in October that year to multiple counts of aggravated assault while armed with dangerous weapons, along with a charge of cruelty to children.

District of Columbia superior court judge Herbert Dixon gave Bell the maximum sentence allowed under the plea agreement she reached with the prosecutors.

According to prosecutors, Bell had gone on a crack binge in the 24 hours before the street festival, consuming 700 worth of the drug. She then placed her seven-year-old daughter in the back seat of her station wagon and headed to unifest, a church-sponsored street festival in south west Washington. At the speed of up to 70mph, Bell made two passes through the area, knocking people to the side and under the car.

A police officer who tried to pull her over said she was laughing as she drove. Her station wagon was finally stopped when officers crashed their scooters under the vehicle and a man jumped through the window to put the transmission in park. No one was killed but 49 people who were injured described in court how they were dragged for several blocks under the car or were thrown into the air by the impact. Most said they felt sorry for Bell.

Antwan Williams, 49, has had four operations on an injured leg and still suffers migraines and flashbacks. "I'd just like to ask her why she didn't stop when she hit the first person", Williams told the judge.

Bell's attorney said she had lived a tortured life, with abusive and absent parents. After eight criminal convictions, Bell appeared to have righted her life somewhat in 2004 when she was on a drug treatment programme. However she later became involved in an abusive relationship which precipitated a drug relapse. Bell said she had attended unifest as a child.

"I am horrified, I ruined such a blessed event", she said.
(Source <u>cnn.com</u>)

Looking at the story of Bell very well, you will discover one good reason you must strive to have a good home and become a great parent. Her attorney said "she had lived a tortured life, with ABUSIVE and ABSENT parents". And like her parents, she got entangled in an abusive relationship and that affected her psychologically as she relapsed into drug before committing that crime that would make her live the rest of her life behind bars. If you were not ready to do everything to make your marriage work initially, read this lady's story again.

Do everything to make your marriage healthy; never give the world another Tonya Bell.

The Heritage Foundation in America made this report public recently:

1. The impact on the emotional, financial and physical well-being of a divorced couple is immediate and essentially negative.
2. It takes many years for both ex-spouses to recoup emotionally, financially and psychologically from the impacts of their divorce.
3. Regardless of age, many children of divorced parents have never fully overcome the adverse effects of family disruption.

Re-Married Couples and Step-Families

1. Re-married couples experience a much higher rate of divorce than first time married couples.
2. Couples in second marriages and step-family members experience another range of emotional complexities and relational challenges.

Out of Wedlock Birth and Single-Parent Families

1. Single mothers and children from unmarried homes are likely to be in poverty or near poverty level for an extended period of time.
2. Women raising children out of wedlock are less likely to find a marriageable mate than single, childless women.
3. Children of single parents are more likely to engage in high risk relationship and high-risk behaviours at earlier age, than children by married couples.

Research has shown that both divorce and unmarried child-bearing decrease the economic well-being of both children and mothers. Only 9% of children under the age of six in two-parent households are poor, while 47% of those living in single-mother households live in poverty. More specifically, 45% of children raised by divorced mothers and 69% raised by never-married mothers live in or near poverty. One analysis found that nearly 80% of child poverty occurs in broken or never formed families, and it concludes that more marriages could reduce poverty as much as 25%.

While compared to children in two-parent households, evidence reveals that children in one-parent households are affected in additional negative ways.

4. Children in two-parent households are less than half as likely to have emotional or behavioural problems.
5. Children in two-parent households are a third as likely to use illegal drugs, alcohol, or tobacco.
6. Children in two-parent households are 44% less likely to be physically abused or neglected.
7. Boys in two-parent households are only half as likely to commit crime leading to incarceration in their thirties.
8. Fifteen-year-old girls in two-parent homes are one-third less likely to be sexually active.
9. Children in two-parent households have higher grades, higher college aspiration, better school attendance and lower dropout rate.
10. Children in two-parent households are less likely to cohabitate prior to marriage, become a single parent or teen parent, and become separated or divorced.

11. Children in single-parent households are at greater risk of poor health, poor behavioural and poor educational outcomes.
12. They are also more likely than children in two-parent families to live in poverty, drop-out of school, abuse drugs or alcohol, and exhibit delinquent behaviours.
13. Children who grow up with married, biological parents are more likely to complete high school, have better health and become economically self-sufficient as adults.

The Northwest Marriage and Family Movement in America conclude from its research: "Healthy, strong marriages between a man and a woman are good for adults, essential for children, positive for society" (Source: Chicago Land Marriage Resources Center).

I believe that by now you must have realized the evils a bad marriage can do to you, your finances, health and the life of your precious children.

What will you do now? Divorce should be the last thing on your mind; you should abhor it like a plague because only the devil enjoys it. Your focus should be on how to build a healthy marriage, how to make your marriage work by all means, and how to make the life of your children better by standing up for your marriage, despite all odds.

The need for a healthy marriage cannot be over-emphasized; this is a point on which both the scriptures and modern researchers perfectly agree. Let me show you from the Bible:

*It paves the way for prayer to be answered (Ecclesiastes 4:9-12)
*A bad marriage can hinder prayers (I Peter 3:7)
*It can destroy one's relationship with God (Malachi 2:14-16)
*It can impede one's progress.

The U.S. Department of Health and Human Services and Healthy Marriage Initiatives reeled out the report below, tagged BENEFITS OF HEALTHY MARRIAGE FOR CHILDREN AND YOUTH.

It will surprise you that a non-religious body could document a report that proves what the scriptures have been emphasizing about family life.

BENEFITS OF HEALTHY MARRIAGE FOR CHILDREN AND YOUTH

The following benefits have been discovered through researches for children and youths raised by parents in healthy marriages, compared to unhealthy ones:

-More likely to attend college
-More likely to succeed academically
-Physically healthier
-Emotionally healthier
-Less likely to abuse drugs and alcohol
-Less likely to show delinquent behaviours
-Less likely to be a victim of physical and social abuse
-Have a better relationship with their mothers and fathers
-Decreases their chances of divorce when they get married
-Less likely to contact STDs
-Less likely to remain or end in poverty
-Have better relationships with their children

BENEFITS OF HEALTHY MARRIAGES FOR MEN

Researchers have found many benefits for men who are in healthy marriages, compared to unhealthy ones including the following statistics:

-Live longer
-Physically healthier
-Wealthier
-Increase in the stability of employment

-Higher wages
-Decreased risk of drug and alcohol abuse
-Have better relationships with their children
-Less likely to commit violent crime
-Less likely to contact STDs
-Less likely to attempt or commit suicide

BENEFITS OF HEALTHY MARRIAGES TO COMMUNITIES

Researchers have found many benefits for communities when they have higher percentages of couples in healthy marriages, compared to unhealthy marriages, including the following statistics:

-Higher rates of physically healthy citizens
-Higher rates of emotionally healthy citizens
-Higher rates of educated citizens
-Lower domestic violence rates
-Lower crime statistics
-Lower teenage pregnancy rates
-Lower rates of juvenile delinquency
-Lower rates of migration
-Higher rates of house ownership
-Higher property values
-Decreased need for social services

For your benefits, children and the society, do everything to make your marriage healthy and strong. That is what is called ONE HUNDRED PERCENT MARRIAGE.

The rest of this book is devoted to teaching you how to build this kind of marriage. You will find it practical and interesting; there will be many examples, stories, jokes and living testimonies just to drive home the point that, no matter the state of your marriage, no matter what you scored in the healthy marriage test, it can still be better. Do not crucify, justify or glorify yourself; just make up your mind that you want a better deal in your marriage and you are ready to see it work. Read the book with an open mind, don't argue with facts. Just decide to change. It is well with your home.

CHAPTER 4
PREPARE A SOLID FOUNDATION

One wise man said: "IT'S NOT THE LOAD THAT WEIGHS YOU DOWN, IT IS THE WAY YOU CARRY IT."

If the foundations be destroyed, what can the righteous do? (Psalm 11: 3)

Several years ago in a town in Osun State (South West, Nigeria), the board of elders of a church decided to build a very big church. After a while, they gathered their resources and started the construction of the church building. Along the line, some of their children based in another country at that time arrived home about the time they started the construction. Excited about the project, the children thought it was best to copy the design of the church they saw outside this country. They convinced the elders to build two towers at the entrance of the church and put what they call "city clock" at the top of the towers. They reasoned that people in the town and the neighbouring ones can have a good view of the clock wherever they were.

This they concluded would make their church and town of high prestige. Good idea, you will say.

They did this without considering the original plan and foundations already laid for the building. However they made the adjustments and completed the construction. The two towers stood magnificently at the entrance to the church, with the clock's alarm ringing every hour. It was a pride to the church and the whole community. Neighbouring towns could easily know what time of the day it was.

They set a day for the dedication of the building and towers. It was scheduled for 11am on a Saturday. The whole town had been invited to be there. A lot of people had come from all over the world. The children who came up with the idea had brought their friends in preparation for a glorious event. They had prepared a lot of food and drinks. But disaster struck! Around 9pm the previous Friday, there was a big bang; it resounded, covering several kilometres. The left tower fell together with the left walls of the church – they crumbled. By 6am the next day, a similar thunderous sound shook the ground. The second tower gave way and went down with the right walls of the church. It was a pathetic sight.

Some people blamed the devil, while others pointed accusing fingers at witches and wizards. However, the government of the western region of Nigeria investigated the incident. They discovered that the building collapsed because of faulty foundations.

Like the collapsed building, a bad foundation can cause the collapse of a home, no matter how great the wedding was.

I included this chapter and the next one for the benefit of the singles who may read this book. Read it with care and take appropriate steps if one hundred percent marriage is your desire. Parents reading this book should also use it as a material to counsel their children.

WRONG FOUNDATIONS FOR MARRIAGE
According to the grace of God which is given unto me, as a wise master builder, I have laid the foundation, and another buildeth thereon. But let every man take heed how he buildeth thereupon. For other foundation can no man lay than that is laid, which is Jesus Christ. Now if any man build upon this foundation gold, silver, precious stones, wood, hay, stubble; every man's work shall be made manifest: for the day shall declare it, because it shall be revealed by fire; and the fire shall try every man's work of what sort it is

(1Corinthian   3:10-13).

1.Money: If your marital choice is based on money, you may regret it later. Money does not last forever. Never choose to marry anybody because he or she is rich. *For the love of money is the root of all evil: which while some coveted after, they have erred from the faith, and pierced themselves through with many sorrows* (1Timothy 6:10).

2.Beauty: Beauty does not exist everlastingly. Look beyond the external appearance when deciding on whom to marry. Never marry because of the "container"; please check the "content".

3.Position: No matter the position the person occupies, that is not sufficient in exchange for your destiny. Position in the church, on campus or in the society should not be the basis for your marital choice.

4.Sex: Desire to have sex or the sexy look of a person is also a wrong foundation for marriage; don't base your marriage on it.

5.Desire to travel abroad: A lot of ladies make the mistake of marrying a man that promises to take them abroad. This is totally wrong; your life is too precious to be exchanged for a trip.

RIGHT FOUNDATIONS

1. Genuine Conversion: Take critical look at the spiritual foundation of the person you plan to spend the rest of your life with. Marry only somebody that is genuinely converted, somebody that fears the Lord. You cannot fare well in the hands of the child of the devil; it will be too difficult to do.

2. Maturity: There is time for everything. Become mature before you think of marriage; become an adult physically, spiritually, mentally, emotionally, socially and financially. Marriage is not for boys and girls, it is for people who can shoulder responsibilities, people that can carry the burden of others; be mature.

3. Prayer: Lay a solid foundation of prayer for your marriage. Seek God's face concerning the person you should marry and commit the issue into his hands.

In all your ways acknowledge Him, and He shall direct your paths. Be not wise in thine own eyes, fear the Lord, and depart from evil it shall be health to thy navel and marrow to thy bones (Proverbs 3:6-8).

4. God's leading: The scripture above commands you to acknowledge God so that he can direct your

path. It is not just about praying, it is about listening to and obeying his command. So it is to your advantage when you allow God to lead you into marriage. This guarantees a home devoid of problems and sorrow. But if you fail to acknowledge him, you may prepare for trouble tomorrow.

5. Love: Marry only the person you love and who equally loves you. Love is the foundation of a strong marriage; without it, the family will not stand. Be very sure you marry somebody that loves you; do not negotiate this. Do not marry based on sympathy or driven by pressure. Marry for Love.

6.Godly Character: Critically examine the character of the person you intend to marry. If he or she has fundamental character flaws, do not marry him or her. If you desire a good home, run from anybody that has uncontrollable anger; given to drunkenness, and unforgiving. Someone who fights, lies, steals and is unfaithful should not be your marital mate.

7.Purity: Lay the foundation of your home on purity; flee as from terror from pre-marital sex.

8.Counsel: Seek counsel before you take any step towards marriage. Never do it alone. No matter how wise and anointed you are, you cannot see your back; in the multitude of counsel, there is safety.

9.Godly Courtship: Courtship begins the moment a couple agrees to marry each other until the marriage takes place. Driven by righteousness, pre-marital sex should never be part of a Christian courtship. Rather, courtship should be a time of deep spiritual interactions; a time to dig into the life of your partner, to learn about him, his past, plans, ambitions and, of course, ministry. It is a time to know each other's friends and families.

10. Glorious Marriage: Lay a solid foundation for your marriage by having a godly wedding. Cohabitation before wedding is unbiblical. Do everything right; fulfill all righteousness if you want God's blessing upon your home.

CHAPTER 5
BEDROCK OF ONE HUNDRED PERCENT MARRIAGE

There are many factors that will determine whether your marriage will end up a one hundred percent marriage or not. I call them "bedrock" because they combine together to determine the state of your marriage, now and in the future. Surprisingly, they are not what you think. They are:

1) YOUR RELATIONSHIP WITH GOD

   The Lord is my shepherd; I shall not want. He maketh me to lie down in green pastures: he leadeth me beside the still waters. He restoreth my soul: he leadeth me in the paths of righteousness for his name's sake. Yea, though I walk through the valley of the shadow of death, I will fear no evil: for thou art with me; thy rod and thy staff they comfort me. Thou preparest a table before me in the presence of mine enemies: thou anointest my head with oil; my cup runneth over. Surely goodness and mercy shall follow me all the days of my life: and I will dwell in the house of the Lord forever (Psalms 23:1-6 KJV).

Your relationship with the Lord ultimately determines the state of your marriage. It is only the shepherd that knows where *green pastures* and *still waters* are. He is the only one that can nourish your soul in marriage. He is the only one that can set a table before you in your house, even in the presence of your enemies. He is also the one that can make your joy and love to run over, goodness and mercy to follow you all the days of your marital life.
- Surrender your totality to the shepherd.
- Be a Bible student.
- Live on the truth of the word of God.
- Spend time with the shepherd daily in prayer.
- Live in holiness and righteousness.

2) WHO YOU ARE
Your personality affects your marriage and determines what happens there. Couple often blames each other for the state of their marriage. The truth is you will only attract someone like you. If you are a lukewarm Christian, you will attract a lukewarm

Christian like you. Likewise, if you are immoral, people that live for God will look too spiritual to you, hence they will not interest you. The best way to get the right PARTNER is to be a right PERSON yourself. Check the following:

-Your Character: If your character is not satisfactory your marriage can never be alright. You need to deal with your character lest it brings your wedlock to a deadlock.
-Your Attitude: Your attitude to God, money, people, time, food, sex, work, friendship, conflict, vision, in-laws and so on will ultimately affect your marriage. If your attitude is negative, your marriage will suffer.

3) STATE OF YOUR MIND

And the Lord came down to see the city and the tower, which the children of men builded. And the Lord said, Behold, the people is one, and they have all one language; and this they begin to do: and now nothing will be restrained from them, which they have imagined to do Genesis 11:5, 6 (KJV).

Your mindset matters. Nothing can stop you from achieving what you determine to have once it is etched on your heart. If you have a wrong mindset about marriage, nobody can really help you except he can change your mind.

So you need to think right about the opposite sex, in-laws, marriage, parenting and so on. Little wonder the Bible commands you to keep your heart with all diligence, because everything about life flows from there.

Keep thy heart with all diligence; for out of it are the issues of life Proverbs 4:23 (KJV).

4) STATE OF YOUR MOUTH
Your mouth matters in your marriage. Whatever you say about your spouse and marriage will ultimately affect them. If your mouth is horrible your marriage will be terrible; if you speak well, you will live well in marriage and have a great family.

5) YOUR PICTURE OF OPPOSITE SEX
Your mind set about the opposite sex matters. To some men all women are bad and are necessary evil. All they know is money; in fact, they are gold diggers. And to

some women, all men are evil. They are all bully and terrible. Anybody that wants to marry them should prepare for war. This kind of mindset will only set you up for a battle in marriage. To have a hundred percent marriage, your mindset must be right about the opposite sex. You must note that not all men are bad; likewise, not all women are terrible. Make up your mind that you are going to marry the best from among the opposite sex and you are going to give your marriage the best.

6) WHO YOU DECIDE TO MARRY
Your marital destiny will also be seriously affected by your choice of life partner. While it is in your power to marry whosoever you wish, let it be known to you that, you alone will bear the consequences of your choice. Abigail decided to marry the wicked, drunkard and godless Nabal. It was her choice and she lived to face the consequences of getting married to a man like that, a man God had to kill by himself (1Samuel 25: 9-38). Be careful of who you join your destiny with. Your happiness and fulfillment in life depends on it. Do not marry an unbeliever, drunkard, angry man; wicked, foolish, fornicating, dishonest, lazy,

vision-less person. Somebody you cannot trust, who does not love you; stingy, extravagant, occult person.

7) THE FOUNDATION YOU LAY
If the foundations be destroyed, what can the righteous do? (Psalms 11:3 KJV) If you lay a wrong foundation, you will have a wrong marriage. If you lay a shaky foundation, you will have a shaky marriage. If you want a hundred percent marriage, you will have to lay an excellent foundation for it. This includes prayer, obedience, knowledge, patience, love, counsel, divine direction, purity and wisdom.

8) THE PREPARATION YOU MADE
Your preparation will affect your marriage. Marriage is like sitting for a school exam. If you have prepared well, you will have a great result. If not you will fail woefully. Unlike a school exam however, your preparation for marriage should involve spiritual, physical, mental, financial, social, emotional and intellectual preparations. Every job is twice difficult when you fail to prepare for it. Rehearsals make a singer; gym work out makes a boxer; regular training makes an athlete; practice makes

perfect. Preparation is the mother of success in any venture, marriage inclusive. *The ants are a people not strong, yet they prepare their meat in the summer* Proverbs 30:25 (KJV). You won't need any devil to destroy your marriage if you go into it without adequate preparation. You are the devil already, recruited for the job. Prepare sufficiently for every phase of your marriage.

The preparations of the heart is man, and the answer of the tongue, is from the Lord Proverbs 16:1 (KJV).

9) YOUR WILLINGNESS TO LEAVE AND CLEAVE
Your willingness to leave your father and mother and cleave to your spouse will also determine how your marriage will end. If you are already married to your parents and you are not ready to 'divorce' them, then you are not ready for one hundred percent marriage. A great marriage will result from leaving parents to cleave exclusively to one's partner physically, mentally, emotionally, financially according to the injunction of the Bible.

Therefore shall a man leave his father and his mother, and shall cleave unto his wife: and they shall be one flesh (Genesis 2:24 KJV).

CHAPTER 6
MARRIAGE IS A
LOVE AFFAIR

As the lily among thorns, so is my love among the daughters. As the apple tree among the trees of the wood, so is my beloved among the sons. I sat down under his shadow with great delight, and his fruit was sweet to my taste. He brought me to the banqueting house, and his banner over me was love (S O S 2:2-4).

A young couple went to visit the husband's grandfather as they used to do before they got married. As they parked their car, the old man happily watched them from his garden. But to his chagrin, the young man alighted from the car, and ran to meet him, leaving behind his wife, baby and the bag of gifts they brought for him. The young husband embraced him joyfully but the old man was not enthusiastic. He asked after the whereabouts of the wife and the young man replied, "She's in the car. She is coming with a gift for you". In anger, the old man asked, "Is that your wife or your maid?" "Haba! Granpa; that is my beloved wife, not my house maid" was the replied he got. Sadly, the old man said, "You treated her as your maid; you do not respect her or show her love. Go back to the car, help her with the bag or with the baby; treat her like a lady. When you used to come here with her before your wedding, you used to hold her hands, help her with her bags, and treat her with love, respect and honour. Now that you are married to her, you stopped all the kind actions you usually did and now overlook little courtesies. You've forgotten that MARRIAGE IS A LOVE AFFAIR".

Like this young man, most of us easily forget that marriage still remains a love affair, a romantic relationship. We abandon love, forsake companionship, overlook friendship, avoid courtesy and destroy romance. Most people treat their spouses with the highest level of disregard; they cut them to sizes with their mouth. Couple embarrasses each other in the public; call each other names and give little or no attention to each other, displaying a high level of disaffection.

WHAT MANNER OF MARRIAGE IS YOURS?
Let us classify marriages based on romance:

1.Traumatic marriages: In this kind of marriage, couple lives like cat and dog. They see each other as enemies. They fight and embarrass each other.

They overlook past good deeds; they nag, refuse to forgive, deny each other sex, retaliate, and hate each other with a passion. Above all they keep records of hurts, keep malice, and they prefer staying in the office than at home. A traumatic marriage makes nobody happy except the devil; the woman is not at rest, the husband is tensed up, the children live like refugees, and God is not at home in the house.

2. Electronic marriage: This is the kind of marriage where the husband and wife stay in different towns for one reason or the other but only communicate through phone calls, E-mails, text messages, fax, and letters. No matter the number of phone calls and mails a couple send to each other daily, it does not equate a face to face discussion, recreation, companionship, and friendship. Marriage suffers a great deal when couples are not together; it allows romance to die, gives room for unfaithfulness, distrust, loneliness, separation, resentment, and anger.

3. Plastic Marriage: Most couples were friends before they became lovers but, after the wedding, they abandoned friendship, companionship, romance, and affection. They become routine husbands and wives; the man gives the money, the woman does the cooking. They talk only on general things like the children's school fees, electricity

bills, food allowance; no love, no attention and affection. They make love like goats do; without passion, without interaction, no communication. They fight seriously before 'he' can "conquer" his woman. Most couples are not friends; they only have a "matrimonial relationship". They live together as co-tenants, or close neighbours; intimacy is abstract. In fact, some live together as total strangers, without love, openness, acceptance and celebration.

4.Romantic Marriage: This is a marriage that involves deep intimacy, recreation, interaction, affections, romance, passion, friendship, companionship and total commitment. This is a marriage that still remains a love affair despite the years. It is the only marriage that greatly satisfies God.

MAKING YOUR MARRIAGE A LOVE AFFAIR

Behold, thou art fair, my love; behold, thou art fair; thou hast doves' eyes within thy locks: thy hair is as a flock of goats that appear from mount Gilead. Thy teeth are like a flock of sheep that are even shorn, which came up from the washing; whereof every one bear twins, and none is barren among them.

Thy lips are like a thread of scarlet, and thy speech is comely: thy temples are like a piece of a pomegranate within thy locks. Thy neck is like the tower of David builded for an armoury, whereon there hang a thousand bucklers, all shields of mighty men. Thy two breasts are like two young roes that are twins, which feed among the lilies (S O S 4:1-5).

1. Remain friends: Never outgrow friendship, remain connected. Care, love, jokes, play, are all acts of friendship; be committed to them.

2. Spend quality time together: Togetherness is said to be the soul of marriage. In fact, the best way to spell love is T-I-M-E. Never allow the demands of modern day life squeeze the life out of your marriage. Spend quality time together. Talk. Keep on talking, express your minds in love, let there be deep and heartfelt discussions. Be open to each other. Talk; look straight into each other's eyes. Talk, touching each other; be intimate. Be lovers.

3. Create an atmosphere for romance: Be vulnerable, jovial; laugh easily, be playful like a child. Look forward to being together, love each other's company. Don't be tired of romance, be creative and thoughtful; just do it.

4. Create time for recreation: Your marriage cannot thrive if you are always on the fast lane of life. Slow down; create time to rest, relax and play. When last did you relax together? When last did you to play together? Communication can only get to the peak and you can remain intimate as you relax together.

5. Give gifts: Lovers exchange gifts. Give gifts to your spouse; don't wait till his or her birthday. Do it now! Go ahead; celebrate your spouse through giving. Give generously; one good way to show love is to give. *For God so loved the world and gave His only begotten son...* John 3:16.

7. Celebrate each other: Be excited about each other. Look forward to meeting each other and be glad to be together. Be proud of each other, and use every opportunity to celebrate each other with excitement.

8. Celebrate special days: Your spouse's birthday should not go unnoticed; celebrate it. Make it the most important day in your life and do everything to always make it remarkable.

Also don't forget your wedding anniversary, father's day, mother's day and some other special days in your life. Do everything to celebrate them, just for your spouse.

9. Be generous with appreciation: Everybody loves to be appreciated; do it to your spouse, do it now! Appreciate everything and stop being critical. Women get better when they are appreciated for good looks and good food.

10. Forgive generously: For you to retain the fire of love in your marriage, you must be ready to be a generous forgiver. No matter how good your marriage is, no matter how strong you are as a Christian, you will still offend each other. That is why you must cultivate the habit of quick and total forgiveness.

11. Let there be oneness: Do not just be together, be one. Togetherness is physical; oneness is a state of mind. Let there be a unity of purpose, unity of direction, and unity of focus.

12. Be Committed to each other: No matter what happens, be committed to each other. Never think of calling it quits. Stay long enough in that marriage to make it a success; be faithful and be fruitful.

13. Be ready to serve and make sacrifices: Do not be content with what your spouse will do for you; rather, look out for what you can do for him or her. Serve your spouse when it is convenient or when it

is not. Learn to sacrifice; do not always be at the receiving end, be at the giving end.

14. Be selfless in your thinking and actions: Do everything without selfishness. Be selfless; put your spouse first in everything. Do not say "myself", say "you"; not "mine" but "ours". Look out for the good of your partner, by all means; celebrate each other's existence.

15. Operate in love: Let love motivates whatever you do. Be clothed with love. Talk in love and if you must be angry, do so in love. If you must 'fight', do it in love. And if you must misunderstand, it must end in understanding.

16. Be playful: This is where couples miss it. Many couples do not play together. That is why the house is always hot and tense. Be playful at home; never be too serious. Relax. Throw pillows at each other at pillow fights. Hide behind a door and jumping out unexpectedly to frighten your spouse. Be creative about this. Men especially should not allow their ego to deprive them of the enjoyment in being playful with their wives. This will in no way demean them; it will only show them to be real men.

17. Let there be humour: Crack jokes, laugh

heartily. It is good for your health and marriage. Laugh over mistakes; make positive jests of each other. Light up the whole house and make it a place to be.

18. Be generous with touching: Touch each other; make it your habit to touch each other as you talk. Cuddle as you sleep, massage each other's body. Sleep on the rug or sofa with your spouse's head on your lap. Walk the street hand in hand. At home rest on each other's shoulder and make your home the best.

19. Give love-making a chance: Do not 'rape' each other; don't just have sex, make love. Get fulfillment in your bedroom life; celebrate sex in your marriage. It is a gift from God. Do not allow it to become a problem in your marriage.Talk about it; improve yourself. Learn, read books, go for counsel. By all means, be a better lover in the bedroom.

CHAPTER 7
MARRIAGE IS MORE THAN A LOVE AFFAIR

Better is the end of a thing than the beginning thereof: and the patient in spirit is better than the proud in spirit (Ecclesiastes 7:8).

Marriage is not just a love affair; it is deeper than that, it is a commitment - a life time decision to love, care for, be kind to and to have sex with only one person, no matter what happens for the rest of your life.

The vow you made on the day of your wedding is the beginning of many other vows and commitment you need to make. Note that the wedding certificate you were given is not a driver's license; it is a learner's permit. That means you still have a lot to do, to learn, and a lot of commitment to make. It will do your family a lot of favour if each person in the marriage can make this commitment individually and as a couple:

Commitment 1: I (we) will make God the head of this marriage. Whatever is not found in this book (Bible) I (we) will not do.

Commitment 2: I (we) will (shall) be a positive partner(s) in this marriage. I (we) will do everything possible to make this marriage succeed.

Commitment 3: I (we) will never use the word 'DIVORCE' in this marriage. I (we) will never think of it, talk of it, or use it as a threat. I (we) would rather affirm my (our) love no matter what happens.

Commitment 4: I (we) will be committed to my (our) marriage vows. I (we) will never have sex with another man or woman as long as my husband or wife lives. I (we) will get every sex l (we) desire from my wife or husband.

Commitment 5: I (we) will be committed to romance and good sex-life in my (our) marriage. Wife - I will not deny my husband sex. I will even invite him for sex once in a while and eagerly do it with him. Thus I will get involve in sex only in marriage and make it thoroughly interesting or my husband.

Husband - I will support my wife in household chores and baby-sitting, so as to show that I am a great husband. I will be skillful in the bedroom; I will make sure my wife really enjoys sex by going for long foreplay and devising more ways to make each moment of love-making an unforgettable one for her.

Commitment 6: - I will never refer to old issues; as soon as we discuss them, I will never mention them again.

Commitment 7: I (we) will not go to bed with offence in my (our) mind and will not keep a record of wrongs. The sun will not set on my (our) grudge.

Commitment 8: I will love my wife or husband no matter what happens.

Commitment 9: I will always say positive things to my husband/wife.

I will always say "I love you", "you are the best", "you are beautiful", and ''you are handsome" and so on.

Commitment 10: I will praise, appreciate and commend my wife or husband at least once in a day.

Commitment 11: I (we) will allow God to use me (us) for the betterment of my (our) marriage.

Commitment 12: I will always honour and respect my wife or husband. I will never disrespect or embarrass her or him, especially in the public.

Commitment 13: I (we) will never report my wife or husband to friends, family members and neighbours.

If I (we) need help at all, I (we) will talk to my (our) Pastor or Christian marriage counsellor who will be unbiased and give counsel based on biblical principles to help me (us) build a better and stronger marriage.

Commitment 14: I (we) will be committed to change any bad character, manners, or habit, that is detrimental to my (our) marriage.

Emotions like anger and acts like stinginess, lies, laziness, perfectionist tendency, malice, nagging, selfishness, shall be dealt with.

Commitment 15: I (we) will make my husband/wife my priority. My spouse will be number one in my life after God. I will direct all my attention and affection towards him or her. I will invest time, money and everything into my (our) marriage.

Commitment 16: I (we) will forgive and reconcile with my spouse, no matter how hurt I am.

Commitment 17: I (we) will apologize and say 'I am sorry' to my wife or husband when I offend her or him.

Commitment 18: I will cross to the land of marriage and break the bridge behind me; no looking back, no turning back, no divorce.

Commitment 19: I will be open to my mate and will not keep any secret from my spouse.

Commitment 20: I (we) will provide for my (our) family.

Commitment 21: I (we) will be committed to positive communication in my (our) marriage.

Say these to each other three times, the husband first then the wife. Thereafter, the both of you hold the book and say it together three times. Embrace, kiss each other and pray together as you hold each other. Re-affirm your love to each other and give glory to God for bringing you together. MAKE SURE YOU REPEAT THIS VOW AT THE BEGINNING OF EACH YEAR.

STAND BY IT

Making commitments and standing by it is the hallmark of a great man and virtuous woman. Defend your commitment, stand by your vow; it will keep your home stabilized, and make you live a great life. Your commitment will commit God to your life and family; your commitment will bring peace, strengthen love in your marriage and establish your home. No marriage can survive without the commitment of the parties involved. No home can move forward except partners decide to be committed to God, their marriage vows and themselves. There is no greater damage that can be done to a marriage than to fail to be committed to it.

Do not take marriage an ordinary duty or a love affair without commitment. I think you will agree with me that marriage is a love affair with a deep heartfelt commitment to each other.

CHAPTER 8
HOW TO USE THE MICROSCOPE IN YOUR MARRIAGE

Let thine eyes look right on, and let thine eyelids look straight before thee (Proverb 4:25)

A microscope is a scientific instrument that makes small objects look bigger so that you can examine them more carefully.

You may wonder what a microscope does in a marriage. A microscope operates in a marriage when a couple focuses on things that are irrelevant and fail to give attention to things that are relevant. It is similar to a situation where while expected to conduct a research on Specimen A you go ahead and put your microscope on Specimen B. I need not to tell you that you will get wrong conclusions.

Where not to put the microscope

1. Never put it on your good deeds, strong point or beauty.

It is not good to eat much honey, so; for men to search their own glory is not glory Proverbs 25:27. The Bible says for you to talk and brag about your glory is not glory, it is pride.

Many men often talk about their strong points, to spite their spouse. This unbecoming act has created negative feelings in many marriages. That is why I warn you against it.

STOP BRAGGING: "IF NOT FOR ME…", "YOU NEED TO THANK ME FOR THAT", "I DID A NICE JOB THERE", and "I TOLD YOU IT WON'T WORK", "I SAID IT". The list is endless.

2. Do not use it on your spouse's weaknesses. Talking often about your spouse's weaknesses will likely make them look bigger than normal. Instead, make it a prayer point; do not weaken your spouse by talking about his or her weaknesses.

3. Do not use it on your past mistakes. Talking often about the past mistakes of your spouse can easily destroy your marriage. A man was fond of referring to his wife's sexual immorality which she carelessly fell into when she and her boss travelled on an official assignment. If the woman stayed a little late in the office the man would say, "I don't know if you have started with your new boss, like you did

with your former one". This continued for years until the woman could not bear it again. She got frustrated and walked out of the marriage. It was then the man realized his error, retraced his steps and begged the woman to return.

4. Do not use it on what you have done for your spouse. It is good that you have done something good for your spouse but do not make an issue out of it. Marriage is all about doing good things for each other; there is no big deal about that. Do you help him pay the house rent? Have you not heard about a woman that built the house where she lives with her husband in the name of her husband and hers? You sponsored her through the university? So what? Have you not heard about a man who resigned from his place of work so as to have sufficient time to take care of his sick wife? Whatsoever you do in that marriage, do it for God and stop making noise about it, or telling anybody that cares to listen what you have done for your spouse. It is foolish and childish attitude. What have you done that others have never done before?

5. Never use it on the past failures of your spouse. Stop talking about his or her past failures. It makes the failure to repeat itself and become a mountain to your spouse.

6. Never put it on your errors. Let past be past. Do not be so attached to your past that you allow it to tie you down. Liberate yourself from your past and make yourself prepared for the future by making the most of today. Note that mistakes of yester-years are not big enough to stop the beauty of your greater tomorrow.

How to use it
1.Use it on what God has done for you in your marriage. Talk about it, praise and appreciate God about it. Count your blessings, name them one by one, and it will surprise you what the Lord has done. Many of us forget His benefits, his healings, provisions.

Bless the Lord, Oh my soul and FORGET not all His benefits who forgiveth all thine iniquities, who healeth all thine diseases who redeemeth thy life from destruction, who crowneth thee with loving-kindness and tender mercies, who satisfieth thy mouth with good things, so that thy youth is renewed like eagles Psalm103:1-5.

2. Put it on your spouse's good deeds. Never underrate the good deeds of your spouse; celebrate and appreciate them. Never make the mistake of seeing them as your right, let it look like a privilege

before you. Have you not seen men and women that are being denied of their right by their spouses? Appreciate your spouse for doing a nice job. Do it now! He pays the house rent and the children's school fees. Appreciate him generously. She cooks a good meal or allows you to sleep with her. Wonderful! Commend her for that; do not see it as one of those things. Appreciate your spouse for every good deed.

3. Put it on your weak points. It is very easy to ignore your mistakes and focus on the mistakes of others. Do not make this mistake; rather, find your error. Fight, focus on, finish it and liberate your home from errors.

4. Put it on your spouse's qualities. She is a good cook. She serves the Lord well. She is a prayer warrior. Appreciate her. He is a good leader, a generous man, diligent, and focused; praise him. Do not allow outsiders to see these qualities before you do. Put the microscope on your spouse's qualities. Note and celebrate them. Unless you do this, they may   depreciate.

5. Your duties that you fail to do. Never neglect your duties and fail to do them. Never ignore the needs of your spouse; provide for, protect, defend, and support your spouse by all means. Do your duty.

6. Put it on your spouse's good looks. The grass always looks greener on the other side of the fence. It is always difficult for many people to see the beauty in their spouses. A wise man once said, "Marriage can be compared to a case whereby you go to a restaurant with friends, you make your order, and they make theirs, but when the order arrives, it is possible to envy them thinking they ordered better meals than yours if you are a person that lacks the spirit of contentment." There was something you saw in that fellow or lady before you decided to marry him or her. Keep on celebrating those things, put the "microscope" on them.

Celebrate your spouse; believe me, your wife is the most beautiful woman in the world. She is just your size; anybody that is taller than her is too tall, anybody that is shorter than her is too short. Not too dark, and not too fat, she is only full (not fat), showing evidence of good nourishment, demonstrating the glory of God in her body, no complaints. Look at her face, and her body, if she is fat, say "thank God for giving me a full and flourishing wife". If she is slim, never use the word skinny, rather say, "She has the stature of a model". Never lust after any other man or woman; be satisfied with what God has given you.

CHAPTER 9
TOTAL
ACCEPTANCE

For we dare not make ourselves of the number, or compare ourselves with some that commend themselves: but they measuring themselves by themselves, and comparing themselves among themselves, are not wise (2cor 10:12).

A man attended his son's graduation ceremony but was disappointed because though the son did very well, he did not win any prize as the best student in any of his courses. This really infuriated the father. The boy sat next to him as he mocked him. Anytime the name of the best student in any course was called, the father would stand up, clap and say, "That is a great son, unlike some ordinary ones" referring to his son. He did this throughout the ceremony and it made the son feel very bad. As they were going back home in the father's rickety car, anytime a good car overtook them, the boy would jump up, clap his hands and say, "That is a great father, unlike some ordinary men with rickety cars". This really got the father annoyed, but he realized that he initiated the cycle. In fact, he had to beg the child to stop talking and he apologized for his mistakes.

A MATE YOU DO NOT ACCEPT YOU CAN NOT RESPECT

Accepting each other is a strong foundation for a solid marriage; it is the first course in the school of marital success. You cannot respect a mate you fail to accept.

"THE GRASS ALWAYS LOOKS GREENER ON THE OTHER SIDE OF THE FENCE".

Unless you make up your mind to accept your spouse, you will always be bitter whenever you are together.

A set of teenagers were given a plain sheet of paper to write out the things they did not like about their bodies. Some of them wrote "I'm too short", some "I'm too tall", "my breast is too big", "my breast is too small", "I'm too slim", and "I'm too fat". The pastor that came to teach them about self-esteem, with their permission, read it to their hearing. It shocked all the "fat" girls that the slim girls wanted to be fat, while the slim girls were surprised that fat girls wanted to be like them. The minister then told them, "You are good the way you are; it is only that the grass always looks greener on the other side of the fence".

There is no better wife like yours; there is no man more handsome than your husband. Please, believe me. Anybody that is shorter than your husband is too short, anybody that is taller than your wife is too tall; your wife is the most beautiful girl in the world. Just believe me and you will see your marriage coming out of the woods.

One thing that baffles me about marriage is that the things that attracted people to their spouses before marriage are the same things they complain about when they get married. A man attracted to a beautiful lady may say some good things about her and later say another thing in marriage.

Before Wedding	In Marriage
1. She is a good cook.	She spends too much time in the kitchen.
2. She loves children.	She spends too much time with the children
3. She is religious.	She spends too much time in church.
4. She has feminine tenderness.	She looks too weak.
5. She listens always.	She lacks ideas of her own.
6. She is generous.	She is extravagant.
7. She is calculative.	She is too slow.

8. She is a good talker.	She is a talkative.
9. She is slim.	She is skinny.
10. She loves God	She is a religious bigot, a fanatic.
11. She is a good dresser.	She is extravagant in dressing.
12. She has good taste.	She has high taste.
13. She is robust.	She is too fat.
14. She is black and shiny.	She is too black.
15. She loves her mother.	She is soul-tie with her mother
16. She is homely.	She is unattractive and unfriendly.
17. She is economical.	She is stingy.
18. She talks wisely.	She is proud.
19. She is industrious.	All she knows is her job.
20. She is a deep thinker.	She is too quiet.

Likewise a lady may say beautiful things about a young man she desires before marriage and then turns around to say something else while in marriage with him.

Before Wedding	In Marriage
1. He has leadership attributes.	He is domineering.
2. He is very strong.	He is too hard.
3. He has financial	He is a miser.
4. He has vision	He is a workaholic.
5. He is productive	All he knows is his work.
6. He is masculine	He is rough.
7. Watching T.V is his hobby.	He is married to his

	television.
8. He is sociable	He is not homely.
9. He is popular among his friends.	All he knows are his friends.
10. He does night shifts.	He is a night crawler.
11. He is full of wisdom.	He feels he knows everything.
12. He is a no non-sense man.	He is wicked and stubborn.
13. He is religious.	He goes to church too much.
14. He loves his mother.	He has a soul-tie with his mother.
15. He is manly.	He is not romantic.
16. He is romantic.	All he knows is sex.
17. He is slim.	He is skinny.
18. He does everything perfectly.	He is a perfectionist.

I want you to check your present complains. You will discover that they are closely related to what you once admired in your spouse. The difference between then and now is that you accepted your spouse then but have stopped now.

SIGNS OF LACK OF ACCEPTANCE OF YOUR SPOUSE

1. Constant complaints: You have too many things you complain about your spouse.

2. Comparing: You are fond of comparing your spouse with others, whether you say it out or not.

3. Condemning: Outright condemnation is another way to show lack of acceptance.

4.Hate his or her company: You hate his or her company. is a sign that you have not accepted your spouse.

5. Lack of commitment: You will find it difficult to be committed to the person you have not accepted.

6. Lack of homely nature: To feel comfortable and friendly at home with somebody you do not accept is not likely to be your past time. If you do not always want to be at home, then check your acceptability level of your spouse.

7. Desire to change your spouse: If you always desire that your spouse should change in almost everything he or she does, it is a good sign that you are yet to accept him or her.

PICTURE OF YOUR SPOUSE

1. His or her natural self: What he or she is, because of his or her gender, biological make-up, temperament, personality or parental background? This is always difficult to change. It is for your own good to know you cannot change him or her. So accept your mate.

2. Association-carved-images: This is a picture of what your mate has become because of his or her education, church, environment, friendship, books, films, background, and so on.

3. Media picture: This is what you thought he or she was before you married him or her, without knowing that whatever he or she was has its own negative effect. You say "she is so organized" but you never knew she had a perfectionist tendencies.

4. Real picture: This is what he or she is as a result of his or her natural components and association-carved-image. You cannot really discover the real picture until after your wedding. The reason you marry him or her is because of his or her media picture, which may be what he or she portrays knowingly or unknowingly. It could also be what you thought he or she is because of one thing or the other. "This man must be a prayerful man", you think, then you went ahead to marry him because you desired a praying man. You jumped to the conclusion that he is prayerful because of the way he prays in church. You never knew that he was not a man of prayer in the closet. You discovered this after your wedding.

5. Expectation picture: This is what you expect him

or her to be; the picture you have painted in your mind which you expect him or her to match.

6. Distorted picture: Because of your criticism, complain and condemnation, he or she set out to change his or herself to fit into your expectations. This leads to distorted picture of your spouse and it hinders him or her to function at his or her best. Your spouse cannot fit into the new picture you have created for him or her and this will make your spouse operate below his potentials and capabilities. The ultimate result of this is a low self-esteem, loss of identity, frustration, depression, tension and fight back.

OUR MAJOR ERROR
Thinking you can transform your spouse to fit into your expectations is one of the greatest mistakes anybody can make in marriage. It is only the creator that can change an individual; but if you continue, you will create tension in your home. The only favour you can do to yourself, your spouse and your marriage is to accept your partner as he or she is.

WONDERS OF ACCEPTANCE
a. High self-esteem: When you accept your partner, it makes him or her to believe in him or herself.
b. Pay back: The partner that is accepted is likely to return the gesture by accepting his or her partner

too.

c. Love: Acceptance is the mother of love; love is likely to be in the home where the mates accept each other.

d. Peace: There would be no tension at all.

e. Romance: Romance and better sex is likely where there is acceptance.

f. Better marriage: The end result of acceptance is good marriage.

HOW TO ACCEPT YOUR SPOUSE

1. Know that he or she is a creature of God who did not make him or herself and thus should be appreciated.

2. You are not better. Note that your spouse has complains about you that he or she decides to overlook.

3. Know that only mature husbands or wives accept themselves. Baby husbands or wives are fond of complains, comparing and condemning. Which one are you?

4. Pray that God should give you the grace to accept your spouse.

5. Focus on the good aspects of your spouse always.

6. Always appreciate your spouse for his or her good deeds, habits or outlook.

7. Take a decision, a stand to love and accept your spouse.

8. Praise God for giving you such a wonderful man or woman to marry.

CHAPTER 10

HABITS OF HIGHLY SUCCESSFUL COUPLES

He that diligently seeketh good procureth favour: but he that seeketh mischief, it shall come unto him (Proverbs 11:27)

Developing a better relationship or a blissful marriage becomes easier if we can develop what we refer to in the marriage counseling ministry as "Home Builder Habits" (HBH). The opposite of this is the "Home Killer Habits" (HKH). There is no neutral ground between them. You are either a 'HBH' or 'HKH' person. What makes marriage difficult is that many couples have HKH, although they have little knowledge that HKH exits. Unfortunately, very few couples have HBH; no wonder number of divorcees increases daily.

Let's examine some HBH Habits
Love-checked tongue: Let love control your mouth; highly successful couples learn how to say the "bitter truth" in a loving way without hurting their spouses. Do not just talk, talk in love. No matter how angry you are, never speak to hurt, never speak to pull down; let your tongue be a builder at home, never a killer.

Donate pleasure: Most people give only hurts to their spouses, but highly successful couples are pleasure to their spouses. Always ask yourself this question before you do anything: "Is what I'm about to do or say going to cause my spouse pain or pleasure?" If you are sure it will give pleasure, go ahead and do it. A successful marriage is simply a marriage where parties involved have mastered the art of giving pleasure to each other.

Be a round table lover: Never be a battlefield person or a fighter, be a "round table" personality and a lover. Let all the "battles" be fought at the round table. Talk about it, and do not forget the first habit of using a love-checked tongue as you talk it out. You must be a crisis manager; reconcile and never retaliate. Be a peace maker, never a truce breaker. Be a positive partner; learn to listen to your spouse with a positive mind.

Make your spouse number one on your "to do list": Indifference is one of the strongest killers of marriage and couples in bad marriages are fond of committing this great "crime". Most do not think about their spouses and have no plan to be together.

Lack of attention is very dangerous to the success of any marriage. Cherish the opportunity to be with your spouse. Be friends, be a companion and be fond of each other. The time you make available to be with your spouse will show how much you value him or her.

Build two-people's-marriage: Make it your habit never to report your spouse to a third party. Learn to talk about your differences and settle them. Avoid reporting your spouse to your friends, families, parents and so on. It is a sign of immaturity. If you need help, get it from a professional counselor. Your friends and family members should remain what they are; "third party".

Build a marriage of honourables: Honour and respect your spouse; say it, show it, demonstrate it, and never embarrass or disgrace him or her whether he or she is present or not. Never make the great mistake of removing the veil of H and P (Honour and Respect) from your marriage.

Pray together: Make praying together your habit. Pray about everything together. Pray to God, holding each other, pray for each other, pray with each other.

Have a joint vision: Develop a joint vision for your marriage, your home, your children and your future. Write down the vision; nurture them to make them a success.

Create time to be in your own world: Learn how to 'escape' from the children, job, or friends. Switch off the phones and television; be in your own world. Three is a crowd, two is a company.

At this period, talk intimately, touch passionately, it is not a period for sex, it is meant to develop and sustain companionship and if sex happens, why not, go ahead. There is no crime committed.

Celebrate success: No matter how small it is, give glory to God. Make it your habit to share testimonies with each other; then celebrate it. You can give a long kiss, a warm embrace, dinner-out and so on.

Have a pre-planned sex. Use the power of pre-planned sex, discuss about having sex at night, before leaving home in the morning. Make phone calls to remind each other through the day. Joke about it, tease each other about it, and it will amaze you what that will do to your sex life.

Let love be spontaneous. Give room for spontaneous sex; a "quickiee" can be fun-filled. Do not be rigid about your sex life.

CHAPTER 11

BECOMING A SOURCE OF BLESSING TO YOUR SPOUSE

A man that hath friends must shew himself friendly: and there is a friend that sticketh closer than a brother (Proverbs 18:24).

A man who was having a very serious problem with his marriage of 12 years visited his father. He went to him to inform him about his decision to quit his marriage. Before then he had mandated his lawyer to file for divorce.

After listening to his son who was trying to convince him that divorce was the best solution to the pitiable state of his marriage, the father asked him, "Is divorce the will of God for your marriage?" and "Is divorce what you really need?" The man replied that divorce is not the will of God for any marriage and that what he wanted is peace, not really divorce. He sadly added, "I think divorce is the only thing that can give me the peace that I am looking for". I would have loved the marriage to remain intact if there is hope for it. But for this marriage, there is no hope".

His father got up from his chair, went close to him, bent low to touch him as he was seated and told him in a very low but serious tone, "There is hope if you do not lose it. Son, there is hope if you hang it on God; yes there is hope".

The young man disagreed with his father and said, "No! Daddy, there is no hope. I have done everything for Dupe, to make her change. I kept malice, I rejected her food, I refused to make love with her, I have done virtually everything but to no avail. I am tired; yes daddy, I am tired.

Are you giving up so easily?" The father asked.

To this, the young man replied, ''I am not giving up so easily dad; I have been struggling and suffering for the past twelve years. Some drastic actions must be taken, if you don't want me, dead. Dupe is driving me crazy.'' He then burst into tears. The old man allowed him to sob for some time, before he knelt down beside him and asked the questions that turned that marriage around forever. He said, "Son, you have told me all the wrong-doings of your wife, but you have not really told me any of yours. You have told me a lot of your wrong reactions to her misbehaviour but Jide, have you ever considered the possibility that her behaviour may have something to do with you? Have you thought about the possibility that she might be reacting to some bottled-up anger, resentment, and bitterness? Have you considered the fact that she may need your help not your rejection? Have you forgotten that a friend in need is a friend indeed?" When the old man saw that his words were "sinking" into his son, he paused and said, "Son, go back and nurture that young woman, go and be a blessing to her. I know you will have a new wife.''

As he drove home that day deep in thought, Jide said he was ashamed of himself for being selfish, uncaring, unloving, unlovable, and a quitter. He said he then made up his mind to change himself instead of seeking to change his wife. He said he drove straight to a fast food joint, where he had been having his breakfast, lunch, and supper for some time to avoid his wife's meal, this time to buy something for his wife and himself. On getting home, he invited her to come and eat with him. She was so surprised but ate with him, though in silence.

The man said, from that time, he decided to make her happy, by little acts of thoughtfulness, care, attention, acts of consideration, patience, gifts, making supper ready for her without placing any demands on her or expecting anything in return. He did everything to promote peace, happiness, and well-being without worrying about her actions and reactions.

At first, Dupe was skeptical and suspicious of his new behaviour, but as he continued his positive interaction with her, coupled with prayers, she was taken by surprise and started responding positively. This encouraged the man to be more positive and the cycle continued like that until their marriage became better and stronger.

Most of the time we blame our spouses for the state of our marriage, we never bother to look inward to see where we have missed the road. Blame and criticism are two of the easiest things to do, but who will take the blame?

If a hundred percent marriage is your desire, then you must become a blessing to your spouse and you must follow the path of blessedness. You must become less demanding, you must stop asking "what will you do for me?" But rather "what can I do for you?"

Let me ask you: are you a source of blessing or a curse to your wife or husband? Are you a plus or a minus? Sincerely between you and me, are you of a noble character at home? Do you think that your spouse should be solely blamed for the state of your marriage? Have you discovered areas where you need to do a "surgical operation" on your actions, reactions and inactions? Don't you think you need to rise up to become a blessing to your mate?

HOW TO BECOME A BLESSING
TO YOUR MARRIAGE

Take responsibility for the state of your marriage. See the log in your eyes, not the speck in the eyes of your mate. Stop the blame game; say "it is me. Yes, I am the issue. If I change, he or she will change; I have a lot of things to change."

Take a firm decision to stop the downward spiral of your marriage. Never wait for your spouse to take decisions, you take the lead. The more mature person among you should be the first to do that. Are you? Then go ahead; apologize, break the malice, make a positive move, call for reconciliation, let there be ceasefire and let there be truce. Put the devil to shame.

Do everything you know to promote happiness and well-being. No matter what, lift your marriage from the state of despair to happiness. Do anything you can do to make your mate a happy man or woman.

Value your mate. Give high value to your mate, and make this known to him or her always. Help your mate to improve his or her self-esteem. Give honour, recognition, respect; communicate your high regards in secret and in public with your words, actions and reactions.

Give quality appreciation. Emotional health and relationship can be destroyed without appreciation. Appreciation makes one's spouse to feel he or she is worth something, has something of value to contribute, and that their work is being recognized. Every human being desires to be appreciated, give it to your spouse. Be generous about it, nothing is too small to be appreciated, make it his or her daily diet; appreciate everything. Do it now! Stop reading this book, close it, then go and appreciate your spouse. Make a call, send a text, be a blessing. Do it now!

Value your time together. Do everything you can to be together. Avoid the television, phone, computer, and avoid the newspaper just to be together.

Give attention. Never ignore your spouse, give a hundred percent attention; attend to him or her.

Give affection. Show love, say it, do it, do not give him or her any reason to doubt whether you love him or her.

Be a creative lover. Show your love in creative ways, improve your love intelligence, do things to surprise your spouse; this will help to nurture your marriage.

CHAPTER 12

INCREASE YOUR INTIMATE TALKING TIME {ITT}

Pleasant words are as a honeycomb, sweet to the soul, and health to the bones (Proverbs 16:24).

One thing you must never fail to improve and increase in your marriage is your "ITT". It means INTIMATE TALKING TIME.

Many couples have nearly zero ITT level. The level of your ITT will determine the health and strength of your marriage. If you have bad ITT, you will have a bad marriage. If you have an average ITT, prepare for average marriage.

We have different 'times' in marriages. I would like to explain them one after the other.

'ST'- Separated Time: This is the time couples spend away from each other. The higher it grows, the more dangerous it is for the family, because as this one grows, it affects the ITT negatively, thereby affecting the marriage.

'BT'- Busy Time: This is the period the couples are together but get themselves busy with their individual pursuits. Most women get busy at home with children, kitchen, and house chores and so on. Men are more occupied at home by computers, newspapers, books and above all television. In fact, television is the second wife of most men; they are always with the remote control surfing channels. They hardly have the time to talk and listen to their wives, thereby increasing their 'BT' at home. The more BT you have at home, the more problems for ITT and, by extension the marriage.

'QT'- Quiet Time: At this time, couples are not busy. They are together but not talking; they are individually in the world of their own. Deep in thoughts, bottled feelings, and engrossed in their different plans. When QT also increases, it is a danger to the marriage.

NTT - Normal Talk Time: At this level, couples talk about their neighbours, church, food, children's school fees, and bills. They do not open up to each other, they are not intimate, and they do not discuss. They only talk. Improvement of NTT and the elimination QT, BT or ST will in the long run promote ITT.

ITT - Intimate Talking Time: This is what we call the highest romantic communication level; it combines intimacy with communication. Couples that constantly operate at this level will definitely have a glorious marriage while people that fail to get to this level cannot but have a difficult relationship. From counseling experience, we discover that less than ten percent of couples operate at this level, which explains the reason many marriages are crashing while many more are finding family life difficult. Your ITT level will determine to a large extent the level of success in your marriage.

It is like this:
1. High ITT produces a romantic marriage.
2. Low ITT produces a romance starved marriage.
3. Very Low ITT produces a plastic marriage.
4. No ITT produces a traumatic marriage.

The state of your marriage depends on your communication skills.

THE BLESSINGS OF INTIMATE TALKING TIME (ITT)

1. It eliminates arguments.
2. It makes decision-making easier.
3. It builds love and understanding among couples.
4. It sustains a romantic marriage.
5. It enhances closeness, togetherness and fondness.
6. It is the foundation of oneness.
7. It eliminates third parties.
8. It glorifies God in marriage.
9. It enhances a good sex life.

HOW TO INCREASE YOUR INTIMATE TALKING TIME (ITT)

1. Create time to be alone together. Busy schedules and modern day city life is a major killer of communication in marriage. Deliberately create time to be together.

2. Create time to talk. Do not just be together, say "let's talk", turn to each other, choose who is to talk first, and let the person speak without interruption.

3. Listen attentively. Let the other party listen attentively, with eyes on the other partner. Listening is not just about hearing; it is not about contemplating on what to say when the other person

has finished speaking. If you focus on what you are going to say rather than on what the other person is saying, you might miss the important point of the discussion. Listening involves the ears, the eyes, and the mind. It involves concentrating on what the other person is saying that you become more conscious of them than you are of yourself.

4. Play together. Many couples can do anything together but play. That is why many marriages are 'plastic marriages' devoid of love, care, companionship, and romance. They just display the husband and wife, 'bring-the-money, I-cook-for-you, you-eat-and-go" attitude in marriage.

5. Respect each other. Never disrespect your spouse. Honour each other, talk in love, respect each other's opinion and never make disparaging remarks about your spouse.

6. Move closer. Intimate discussion is not done when the wife is in the kitchen and the husband is watching the television. You need to move closer, talk deeply and intimately.

7. Touch each other. Touch each other as you talk. You can drop your hand on each other's lap as well. You may also decide to play with fingers and legs;

this allows your blood to flow in the same direction and it enhances your understanding of each other.

8. Pray together. Praying together as a couple brings togetherness and closeness to God. Couples that often pray together are most likely going to talk freely together and enjoy companionship.

9. Crack jokes. Employ the weapon of humour and jokes; laugh, enjoy each other's company, do not be too serious at home.

CHAPTER 13

HOW TO DEAL WITH YOUR MARRIAGE CRISIS

The beginning of strife is as when one letteth out water: therefore leave off contention, before it be meddled with (Proverbs 17:14).

"The successful marriage does not depend on lack of tension or problems but it depends on establishing a relationship which can stand and overcome those tensions and problems" - Derek Prince

Marriage can run into stormy waters anytime and under any circumstance. How couples handle the situation will show their maturity level, relationship with God, depth, knowledge, patience, love and understanding.

Wrong things to do in time of crises

1. Blame each other. "You ruined our weekend",

"You caused it all", "You make me sick", "Your carelessness caused it", "You see where you landed us", and "It is entirely your entire fault". Statements like these do not get the issues resolved but rather compound them.

2. Criticize each other. "You are too demanding", "You are too fat", "Your fatness caused the sluggishness that made us to miss our flight", "You are a bad cook", "You talk like a fool", and "You are lazy".

3. Get defensive. "That is me", "That is my philosophy", "You can't change me", "That is how my father behaves", "You made me to do it", "You caused it all".

4. Avoidance of the issue. "I do not want to talk about it", "Do not disturb me", "There is nothing you say that can change my mind", "Do not waste your time, I have closed this case".

5. Exaggerate the issue. "You will kill me one day", "There is no devil like you", "I regret I married you", "You always do it", "You can't change", "If you die, I will not mourn you".

6. Generalize it. "Women are the same", "You are a

witch like your mother", "You always do it", "You never listen", "You never do anything right".

7. See it as a war. "I am ready for anything", "Bring it hot, and I will bring it hotter", "I am ready for you", "I will show you who I am".

8. Bring a threat. "I will send you packing", "I will go with my children", "I will divorce you", "I will marry another wife", "I will kill you one day", "You will kill me one day."

9. Finalizing it. "I can never forgive him", "I cannot allow him to sleep with me again", "I'm tired of her", "This marriage is over", "I curse the day I met you", "Marrying a harlot is better".

10. Reference to old issues. "That is what you did ten years ago", "You did it when we were courting".

11. Using abusive words. "I never knew you are this stupid", "The house girl dresses better than you", "I do not blame you, your mother is more foolish than that", "That is how your father killed your mother".

12. Expanding it. "I do not even know whether these children are mine", "My problem is that I did

not marry right", "From the day you entered my life, it has been one trouble after another".

13. Standardizing it. "You always get it wrong", "That is what you always do", "You always get me mad", ''Your food always makes me sick".

14. Distort it. "You have never cooked a good meal in this house".
 Statements like these can destroy any home without notice.

Apart from statements like these, couples involve themselves in a lot of other wrong behaviours like:

1. Beating their wives;
2. Rejecting food, nagging;
3. Reporting to third parties;
4. Refusing to cook for their husbands;
5. Open brawls;
6. Sexual denial;
7. Separation of rooms;
8. Keep malice;
9. Sleeping inside the car;
10. Sleeping in the living room;
11. Avoid going home;
12. "Scape goating " (transferred aggression).

Any person that is involved in any of these is a baby; he or she needs to grow. Unfortunately, many of our couples are in that category, even people that have been married for years.

WHAT TO DO WHEN THERE IS CRISIS

If you are a mature person, if you are a real man or a virtuous woman, then do the following to deal with the crisis. Do not follow the norm but rather:

1. Identify the problem. Get to the root of the problem, locate the cause, be sincere about it, and do not blame anyone.

2. Check where you have contributed to it. Do not defend yourself, examine your own contribution; see the situation from your spouse's point of view.

3. Face it. Face the crisis, do not dodge or avoid it. Give it the attention it deserves, never ignore or avoid talking about it.

4. Fight it. Fight the crisis not your spouse; fight your problem not your mate.

5. Finish it. Put the crisis to an end; avoid referring to it when you have another misunderstanding.

WHAT TO AVOID

-Avoid reporting to third parties, apart from your pastor and counselor.
-Avoid thinking negatively about your spouse.
-Avoid the "fight-to-finish" attitude.
-Avoid building walls; by all means build bridges.
-Avoid cursing, slandering, or abusive words.
-Avoid saying things you will regret later.
-Avoid retaliation.
-Avoid threat and intimidation.
-Avoid separation.
-Never refer to old issues.

NO MATTER WHAT HAPPENS

-Continue to love your spouse.
-Continue to respect and honour each other.
-Pray for each other daily.
-Continue to do your duty at home.
-Continue to talk to each other in love.
-Let togetherness continue.
-Always remember your vows.
-Be committed to your marriage.

EASY WAYS TO SETTLE A DISPUTE

1. See your own part of it. Never lay the blame on your spouse or exonerate yourself. It takes two to

tango.

2. Take responsibility for the state of your home.

3. Listen to your partner. Let your partner talk freely, let him or her talk without intimidation, just listen.

4. Respond positively. No defense, no threat and no game-playing. Respond in love.

5. Look for a win-win situation. Never turn it to a contest; you are not in an Olympic Game. No matter how you resolve the issue, make it a no-victor-no-vanquished situation.

6. No retaliation. Seek to reconcile and re-connect, never revenge; if you revenge you equalize, if you forgive you win.

7. Put your own need aside. Meet the needs of your spouse, be selfless.

8. Keep on talking. If you disagree, keep on talking in love; NEVER abandon it until you are able to resolve it.

9. Pray. No matter the level of your disagreement; dare to pray together. Let the Lord set in, he can still all storms.

CHAPTER 14

GIVE ADEQUATE CARE

And be ye kind one to another, tenderhearted, forgiving one another, even as God for Christ's sake hath forgiven you (Eph 4:32).

There is nothing called love without care. In fact, love is simply kindness and caring. There is no way to have a great marriage than to care. If you remove the care aspect of marriage, what will be left will be disastrous.

Care is in short supply in homes today. That is what makes the home become a battle field. One major void God saw in the life of Adam was lack of somebody to care for him. *And the Lord God said, it is not good for the man to be alone, I will make a help meet* (somebody that can care) *for him* (Genesis 2:18).

To care simply means to be concerned about what happens to someone, because you like or love them.

To care for your spouse simply means you give more attention to him or her, you cater for him or her, and you see to his or her welfare.

How do you care for your spouse? That is what we are going to discuss here.

1. Look out for his or her needs. Most of the time we get engrossed in our own needs, to the extent that we neglect the needs of our mate. To care for your spouse, look out for his or her needs as much as it is within your power to do. Meet the needs of your spouse in the following areas:
-His or her needs for appreciation.
-His or her needs for protection.
-His or her needs for sex.
-His or her needs for attention.
-His or her needs for food.
-His or her needs for support.

Meeting the needs of one's partner is like a good seed, it does germinate to become a great tree bringing good harvest.

2. Be genuinely concerned about his or her Job. Show concern, pray for his or her job and career, do everything to see to it that your mate gets the best out of life.

3. Motivate and encourage your spouse in the face of failure. Stand with your mate both physically and spiritually in time of challenges; never allow him or her to be alone. Men most especially should make their bosom available for the woman to rest in time of trouble; that is what marriage is all about.

4. Be his or her number one nurse in sickness. Stand by him or her in sickness, care for your mate, be with him or her in pains, never be non chalant or indifferent.

5. See to his or her welfare. Either you are at home or not, let your mind be with your mate; send a mail, call, ask how he or she is fairing. Never neglect your spouse, let his or her well-being be your joy.

6. Be his or her chief host in celebration. Join your spouse to rejoice in time of celebration. His or her success should be your success, show true joy and happiness when your spouse succeeds; joy has a way of doubling itself when there is somebody to rejoice with.

7. Never allow depression. Use the weapon of prayers, motivation, scriptures, encouragements, songs, humour and laughter to break the stronghold

of depression in the life of your mate. Never give room for depression, let the joy of the Lord take over in your marriage. ***Rejoice in the Lord always and I say rejoice*** Philippians 4:4

8. Understand your spouse's mood. Never allow his or her head to be bowed, bring light into dull moment. Never ignore obvious sign of sadness, fear, and anxiety on the face of your mate; remember two are better than one.

9. Confront problems and challenges together. To care means to stand with your spouse in time of challenges; pray together, encourage and motivate, defend, assure, and be there for your spouse. It is a privilege to be in a position to support your spouse when storm rages, do not disappoint God at that moment.

10. Understand his or her countenance. Get to know the mood of your spouse. Know when he is happy or sad, do everything to lift up the spirit of your mate always, never give room for gloom. Never allow his or her head to be bowed, be a cheer leader. Be a motivator.

CHAPTER 15

VALUE EACH OTHER

Let no corrupt communication proceed out of your mouth, but that which is good to the use of edifying, that it may minister grace unto the hearers (Eph 4:29).

To value your spouse means to see him or her as somebody very important and useful, somebody you love, respect, and honour. Many people do not value there mates. They find it easier to value other men or women that are not their spouses.

One of the major causes of marital problems is 'valueless mentality'. This is the root of most marriage crisis; the reason why you married your spouse is because you value him or her. Do you say you were in love? Yes you are right. There is no way you can love him or her if you do not value him or her. The main reason you have constant misunderstandings now is because you have lost the value, and he has become any other man or woman to you, or even lower than the house-maid.

Do you value your spouse? If you think you do, then answer the following questions:

1. When last did you buy a gift for him or her (not Christmas or birthday gift)?
   a. This week
   b. Last week
   c. Six months ago
   d. More than a year ago

2. How often do you call him or her in the office daily?
   a. At least thrice everyday
   b. Twice everyday
   c. Once
   d. None

3. When last did you tell him or her "I love you"?
   a. This morning
   b. Last week
   c. Last month
   d. Long time ago.

4. When last did you tell him or her "I value you"?
   a. Today
   b. Last week

c. Last month

d. I have never said it before

5. When last did you take her out on a date?
   a. This month
   b. Last month
   c. Long time ago
   d. Never

6. You embarrass him or her (abuse, condemn or curse) privately or publicly.
   a. Never
   b. Seldom
   c. Often
   d. Constantly

7. His or her picture is with you
   a. As screen saver, on mobile phone, on the table in your office and in your bag.
   b. In your bag only
   c. In the house alone
   d. None

8. How often do you refer to him or her when he or she is not there?
   a. Constantly
   b. Often
   c. Seldom   d.Never

9. How often do you quote his or her words?
   a. Constantly
   b. Often
   c. Seldom
   d. Never

10. How did you celebrate his or her last birthday?
    a. In a special way that he or she enjoys
    b. In a casual way
    c. No celebration
    d. Didn't even remember

Score Card

A	-	10	Marks
B	-	6	Marks
C	-	3	Marks
D	-	1	Marks

Now calculate your score to know how much you value your spouse seventy per cent is our pass mark. Anything below that shows you have a lot of work to do on your marriage to make it a marriage of value.

HOW TO SHOW YOUR SPOUSE YOU VALUE HIM OR HER
-Say it. Do not just tell your spouse "I love you"; say "I value you".
-Show it. Show it by listening to him or her, by

serving and making sacrifices. Show it in your actions and reactions, in your communication, attention, and affection.

-Give gifts. Shower gifts on him or her. It is a sign of your value.

-Place his or her picture in your home, on the table in your office, on the wall, as a screen saver on your mobile phone, and computer system, in your bag, and on the dash board of your car.

-Listen to him or her. Always listen to your spouse, give full attention; avoid the television and newspaper, just to give full attention.

-Call often. Call your spouse often. Send text messages, romantic letters, flowers, E-mails, and cards just to show you care.

-Talk to him or her. Do not just listen; enjoy talking to him or her. Share your vision, your joy, your fear, your plan, your purpose, and your aspirations; give adequate information about your life, talk like friends, gist, and laugh.

-Be homely. Always like to be at home with your spouse, enjoy spending time together, and keep company with your spouse.

-Play together. It is only the person you value that you can play with.

-Consider him or her before you take any decision. Never think like a single person, put your mate into consideration before taking any decision.

-Appreciate. Always appreciate your spouse,

commend generously.

-Celebrate everything about your spouse. Show him or her that he or she is greatly valued.

CHAPTER 16

THINGS YOU MUST GIVE YOUR SPOUSE

A man's gift maketh room for him, and bringeth him before great men (Proverbs 18:16).

Do you really desire a healthy marriage? Are you really sure? Are you ready to give it all it will take? If you have answered yes to all these questions, then let me tell you some things you must give to your spouse if you really want a great change.

1. Your heart. Most marriages started with couple having a deep affection for each other, which they call love. It grew so deep that they felt they could not live their lives without one another, hence they got married. Unfortunately for many, that is where the good story ends. Immediately after "yes I do", the heart is allowed to wander away from each other, and married couples hardly miss each other's presence. In fact, they do feel lonely despite being in the presence of each other. The problem is many couples have invested their hearts in something else

to the detriment of their marriages. Some men invested theirs in jobs, business and ministry, some even in strange women, while women invest their hearts in their children, jobs, and in extreme cases on other men.

These are the reasons many homes are in trouble today. Many hands are joined together but minds are miles apart. If you desire better days in your marriage, then give your heart to your spouse. Let him or her have a room in your mind, give love a chance.

To be sincere with you, there is no way to make your marriage work if your mind is not involved in it. Take the time to clean your mind of all hurts, resentment, unforgiving thoughts, bitterness, anger, and all negative thinking. Give room to positive thinking and imaginations. Learn to celebrate your spouse in your mind, accept him or her totally, and never compare your spouse with anybody. Rather, see him or her as a gift in your life, giving glory to God.

Majority of the crisis in your home started from your mind. If you can liberate your mind and become a positive thinker, then you would have succeeded in liberating your marriage.

2. Your hands. Giving a helping hand to your spouse is another thing you should do. You are joined to each other to fulfill God's purpose for your life, you are to stand with, to defend, protect and support your spouse. Men most especially should know that, house chores and baby-sitting are not labeled "for women only". Husbands should give their support in doing this. There is no way she can do all the house chores- cook, take care of the "kids", then you the biggest "kid" and still have enough strength to be your lover girl in bed. Support her. Changing diapers does not change your title from "Mr" to "Mrs". It only shows how responsible you are as a father.

Likewise, wives should give a helping hand in payments of bills, dues, fees, fares and rents. By all means, support your husband. It will be very wrong for you to go shopping for new clothes, shoes, and bags when the house rent is yet to be paid. Most women can give their bodies to their husband, but not their money. What God has joined together let not money put asunder.

3. Eyes. Find pleasure in looking at each other; looking straight into the eyes of your mate when he or she talks shows how much you value him or her. Men should avoid "wandering eyes", avoid looking

lustfully at other women outside; there is nothing they have that is not available in your beloved wife.

4. Mouth. Give your mouth to your spouse. Talk kindly to him or her, let your mouth build your house; let it bring peace to your home and joy to your spouse. Speak to encourage, motivate, praise, build, and make your spouse happy. Speak the truth always, no slander, no curse or abusive words; let your mouth be a blessing. Colossians 4:6.

5. Ear. Always find time to listen to your spouse. Husbands most especially should know that women love to be listened to. The quietest of all women will become a talkative of some sort when she is with the person she loves and trust. They cannot just stop talking and they love it when they have somebody that listens to them. Everything is important to be told as far as a wife is concerned once she has a husband that will listen. Learn to listen to your wife, even if you think what she is saying is not important. If it is important for her to tell you, then it must be important for you to hear.

6. Time. Musicians use time to make symphony, couples should use their time to make harmony. City life makes it so difficult for couples to spend time together. In fact, an average city couple spends less than three hours together every day. When I say

three hours, I am not saying "intimate hours", because the television, phones, children, computer games, internet and so on will still take a large chunk of the three hours we are talking about. Most couples do not have "intimate hours" for months. They have what I call a routine marriage, boring relationship, one where everyone seems to be in haste going nowhere.

If you want a better marriage, then create better time together. Spending time together should not be a luxury, it should be a necessity. Pray for it, make it a priority, plan for it and do something about it. The lesser time you spend together, the greater injury you do to your marriage.

7. Friendship. Do not just spend time together. Spend time together as friends, talking, playing, sharing gist, joking, praying, and relaxing and so on. There should be no dull moment when you are together. You should be valuable to each other; you should talk and play without inhibitions. Do not just be husband and wife; be friends, be lovers, be intimate.

8. Protection. Do everything to protect your spouse and his or her interests. You must protect your spouse from attacks from in-laws, friends,

neighbours and so on. Never collude with your family or friends to attack or fight your spouse.

9. Money. Be generous in giving. Your family should be number one on your spending plan. *But if any provide not for family of his own and especially for those of his house, he hath denied the faith and is worse than an infidel* 1 Timothy 5:8.

You cannot command the blessing of the Lord if you allow your family to starve. You cannot see his good pleasure if you fail to take good care of your home.

10. Your life style. If your lifestyle and habits are not helping your marriage, it will be wise if you drop them. Your habits are not cast in marble, you can still change and improve; you can become better for the good of your home. If you are lazy, dirty, talkative, get angry easily, hate being corrected, eat too much, keep malice, and nag and so on. Work on yourself. You need to develop yourself, if you want a better home. Anti-marriage lifestyles must also change, such as extravagance, stinginess, night crawling, gluttony and so on.

11. Comfort. Praise, encouragement, comfort, motivation should be part of your gifts to your

spouse. Give them in abundance, never allow them to be in short supply; give generously. They are one of the best things you can give to your beloved husband or wife. Note what Rebecca did for Isaac: *And Isaac brought her into his mother Sarah's tent, and took Rebecca and she became his wife, and he loved her, and Isaac was comforted after his mother's death* Genesis 24:67.

Be a source of comfort to your spouse, encourage him or her. Do everything to make your partner happy.

12. Peace. *Make every effort to live in peace with all men and to be holy, without holiness no one shall see the Lord* Hebrews 12:14.

Make sure you do everything to live at peace with your spouse; no malice, fighting, no quarrels, no nagging, resentment, bitterness, hatred, vengeance, strife. Be a positive partner, take the right step to reconcile, be ready to apologize and be quick to forgive generously, never keep record of offences. Remove anything that can remind you of your hurts; let the Lord take the glory.

13. Affection. Love your spouse generously, do not just love, show it, say it, act it, demonstrate it, make

love happen, make God happy and give love a chance.

Dear friends let us love one another, for love comes from God. Everyone who loves has been born of God and knows God 1 John 4:7.

Strive to love your spouse, destroy everything that may erode your love for him or her. Your marriage cannot survive without love; love your spouse.

14. Kindness and goodness. Kindness is the sincere desire for the happiness of others. Goodness is the activity calculated to advance that happiness. Be kind to your spouse; think of her, think of positive things you can do to make him or her happy. Be good to your mate, do things just as an act of goodness and let your spouse be bold to say you are good.

15. Sex and romance. Do not deprive your partner of your body. In fact, your body belongs to him or her not you (1 Corinthians 7:1-5).

Let your spouse be totally satisfied with love action, romance, and sex. Make sure you improve your sex life and never remain on the same spot. Be better, be creative. Satisfy your spouse.

Please, get a copy of our book *Sexual Fulfillment in Marriage* for an in-depth teaching about sex. Do not allow your sex life to die or become boring. It is a gift from God, use it wisely and let the Lord be glorified.

www.ingramcontent.com/pod-product-compliance
Lightning Source LLC
Chambersburg PA
CBHW020551030426
42337CB00013B/1049